Dear Freckle Face

Mandi Smith

BookLeaf Publishing
India | USA | UK

Presentation by *BookLeaf Publishing*

Web: www.bookleafpub.com

E-mail: info@bookleafpub.com

ISBN: 9789358368833

First edition 2024

DEDICATION

This book is dedicated to the memory of my late husband Rickey Smith, who taught me what matters most in this life. I will always love you, babe.

ACKNOWLEDGEMENT

Thank you to my inner circle, the select few friends and family who have been by my side through it all and helped me become the woman I am today.... you know who you are. I wouldn't be me if not for y'all.

Dear Freckle Face (A Letter to My Former Selves)

To the six-month-old hardhead
who felt the need to prove your independence
by crawling off Grandma Peggy's mattress
and connecting with the hardwood headfirst…..
being first at everything isn't always a good
thing.

To the freckle-faced, four-eyed first grader,
so proud to pedal that little pink bicycle
all the way home

all by yourself
in the bitter winter cold,
then fling it into the yard in frustration
once you reached your destination….
remember home is the place where when you
have to go there, they have to take you in.

To the geeky seventh grader
from the wrong side of the tracks,
so full of unwarranted anger and desperate for
acceptance
she once snorted a packet of Sweet 'n Low
and set her nose on fire for days trying to build
this badass persona….
it's okay to be young and stupid, but it's just as
okay to be yourself.

To the angsty high school junior
who fell in love for the first time,
had her first awkward kiss,
broke up with her boyfriend and swore the world
must be coming to an end
and her heart would never heal….
he was the first, not the last. There will be
others.

To the young lady away at college
and living on her own for the first time,
ready to take on the world,

thinking she knew it all…
with education comes knowledge, but with
experience comes wisdom.

To the chubby grungy redhead
wearing flannel and sneakers,
with a Bud Light in one hand and
a Marlboro in the other….
look to your left. See that young man in the
wheelchair?
He will change your life forever, in ways you
could never comprehend. Give him a chance.

To the twenty-year-old newlywed,
wondering what to say to your husband who was
just wheeled into the room
after losing his right leg…
it doesn't really matter. With cracked lips and
dry mouth, he kisses your face and sobs.
All he wanted was to know you were there.

To the weary-eyed thirtysomething woman
who sits steadfastly at his bedside,
holding his hand and stroking his flat head,
feeling your heart break as you listen to his
ragged breaths
fall fewer and further between,
as you whisper "I love you" and tell him it's
time….

this isn't goodbye. He will always be a part of
you. You wouldn't be you if it weren't for him.

To the middle-aged widow
who has struggled to move forward for twelve
years,
but has tried to rediscover her purpose,
in spite of the obstacles Life has thrown her
way…..
Even baby steps show movement.

You got this girl.
Never forget you're a survivor!

I Am Me

I am the girl that no one gets
The four-eyed freckled geek
I am the one with much to say
Though I'm too scared to speak
I am the girl who sits alone

The one the boys all overlook
I am the girl who spills her soul
Within a spiral notebook
I am the girl that no one wants
The one always picked last
I am the girl that's left behind
Who can't escape her past
I am a little girl no more
At 40+, that's plain to see
But the silent nerdy outcast child
Will always dwell inside of me

Walking the Fine Line

Balance
eludes me,
much like rest.
Just when I
feel it
within
reach
of my
tiny T-Rex arms,
my Sasquatchian feet
slip then

slide,
carrying
me one
giant leap further
away from my
unattainable goal:
moderation.
Impossible
to achieve
for a passionate,
all or nothing
lunatic like
myself.
Gray
doesn't exist
within my box
of crayons, only
black and
white.

Daddy Don't Forget

Daddy,
don't forget
me. I'm still
your little girl.
I may
be
older
now, but
you know I'll
always need you.
You've always
known
the
answer, no
matter the question.
Everything is changing.
I see

the
question
in your
eyes and pray
that God gives
me the
right
answer.
Even when
you cannot remember
me, you are
still my
father.

Dear PaPa

Dear PaPa,

I'm sure you didn't mean it, but you scarred me
for life.
When we were little children, we'd climb in the
pickup with Daddy
and drive to your house. You kept the pantry full
of Little Debbie snacks,
and every time we'd visit, we'd eagerly wait for
that magic moment
when you'd smile and turn us loose in the
cabinets, allowing us to chow down
on your stash of brownies.

When I turned ten years old, battling
prepubescent pudge
and already chunkier than all the girls my age,
we ventured to your house.
Unwilling to wait for your permission, I asked if
I could have a brownie.
Looking me up and down disapprovingly, you
sighed, shook your head,
and asked, "Do you really think you need it?"

I was crushed. My lifelong struggle with my
weight had begun.

****

I remember how every Christmas, you'd give
each of us grandkids a crisp new $5 bill.
Until the number of grandkids exceeded the
number of dollars you had to spare.
I didn't understand why the money suddenly
stopped.
Didn't you still love us?

****

December 1992…

Dad drove to your house to check on you, then
called home in a panic.

He couldn't wake you up. They rushed you to
the hospital up the road.
The family came and went, all hours, day and
night. Dad refused to leave you,
and I refused to leave his side. The next
sixty-some-odd hours are a blur, traces of faces
and voices, trails of shared laughter and tears.
The last time Dad and I went back to see you, I
didn't know what to say. I saw my Daddy cry,
which he never did, as he held one of your hands
and I held the other.
He said his "I love you" and I squeezed your
hand silently, hoping you knew I meant the
words he spoke, I simply had no strength to utter
them.
A single tear fell from your eye.

That's the last thing I remember.

****

I'm so sorry….
I never said I love you,
or I forgive you.
Or even thank you,
for the many things you taught me in life,
both good and bad;
for creating my father,
making him the man he is,

who in turn made me the woman I have become:
a lover, a fighter,
a stubborn-headed survivor.

I love you, PaPa.

The Miracle Boy

'Twas the 9th day of June, the year 1969
A frail boy was born with a wide-open spine
All his nerves were a tangled up mangled up
mess
His chance for survival was anyone's guess
The doctor looked sullen, he spoke in hushed
voice
Advising these parents their most humane
choice
Was to head on back home, leave their new son
behind
And continue with their lives, put him out of
their mind
The boy would be crippled, confined to a chair

His defects would require he need round the
clock care
The poor child would suffer throughout all his
days
And burden his family in unspeakable ways
Aware of the chances their son might not survive
They thanked God for keeping their sweet boy
alive
The young couple pondered the doc's every
word
Trying to make sense of all they'd just heard
They clung to each other in a desperate embrace
Praying for God's wisdom, mercy and Grace
They strode side by side, hand in hand, to the
window
Stopped and stared through the glass at the small
boy below
As mother and father gazed down on their son
They knew in that instant what had to be done
Disregarding each word of the doctor's advice
James and Jo chose the path marked by great
sacrifice
Despite everything that the doctor had said
They would not walk away, nor leave their son
for dead
How much time he had left here, they had no
way to know
So they cherished each day shared with sweet
Rickey Joc

They watched with excitement as their young
son grew
And did things that doctors swore he'd never do
He even surpassed all his own expectations
He refused to be bound by physical limitations
In spite of the challenges Life tossed his way
He was grateful God granted him just one more
day
His forty-three years were a wonderful life
I know because he blessed me and made me his
wife
His journey was brief but his legacy lives on
Inspiring the masses long after he's gone
But had it not been for James and his faithful
wife Jo
And that selfless decision made so long ago
When the two first laid eyes on their bundle of
joy
This world would never have known 'bout The
Miracle Boy

Caretaker's Ballad

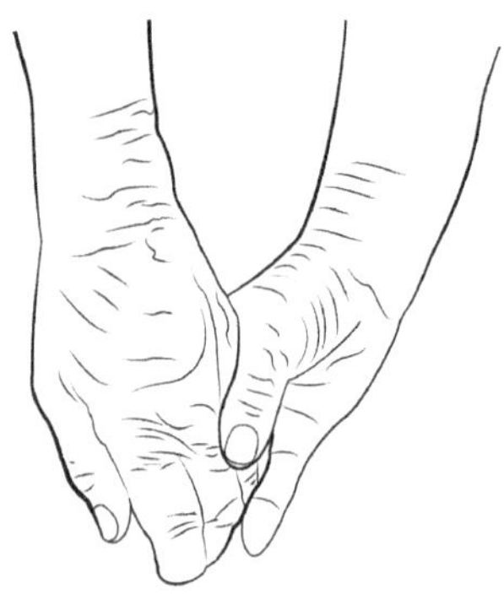

It's late at night but I'm awake
Listening to each breath you take
I lay beside you, stroke your hair
This pain is just too much to bear
I feel my heart breaking in two
Can't face the thought of losing you
I can't let go, I need you here
Life without you is my worst fear
Deep inside, my soul is dying
But I won't let you see my crying
I wait until you're fast asleep
And then I know it's safe to weep
Tears I've stifled for many weeks
Are overflowing down my cheeks
I've watched you suffer for so long now
I want to ease your pain, but how

I cannot bear this cross for you
I feel helpless, hopeless too
I know there's nothing I can do
But watch the light go dark in you
I've seen you fight, you're tough as nails
I wish I could be strong as well
I know I must be brave for you
But I don't have the strength you do
Even in pain, you're full of grace
You wear a smile upon your face
Your flesh is weak, your faith is strong
You've fought and held on for so long
You know a better life awaits
Just beyond those Pearly Gates
I lay my hand across your heart
Preparing for the hardest part
I dry my tears and close my eyes
And force myself to realize
Your body is tired and longs for rest
And I know this is for the best
I wrap you in a warm embrace
Kiss your lips and touch your face
I hold your hand and pull you near
Whisper "I love you" in your ear
You wake and flash your smile my way
You squeeze my hand and softly say
"I love you" with your final breath
Then close your eyes and walk with Death

Without You

An empty bed lays next to me
I reach out where you used to be
My fingers seek but all they find
Are memories you left behind
The tears rain down as truth sinks in
I feel your loss over again
I long to talk to you once more
To ask you what's worth living for
I look around our room and see
Your smiling face stare back at me

I ask your picture on the shelf,
"How can I do this by myself?"
You were my life, my soul, my heart
But now my world's been torn apart
I really need you here with me
You were my strength, my sanity
I don't think that I'm strong enough
To face this life without your love
Without you, babe, I have no clue
Who I am or what I should do
I don't know how to live my life
If I'm no longer "Rickey's wife"
I'm thankful that you're out of pain
And one day I'll be with you again
But there's this selfish side of me
That wants you where you shouldn't be
Back here, beside me, in our bed
Not with the Lord up there instead
I feel so lost without you here
I pray you won't forget me, Dear
You will forever be my heart
Long after our death do us part
I pray for a better day tomorrow
That's filled with less of this great sorrow
I hold out hope that each new day
Will somehow take this pain away

A Widow's Christmas

'Twas the night before Christmas and I lay
awake
Praying to God to end my heartache
Longing to lay with my husband again
Instead sleeping over at the home of my friends.
They had all gone to sleep when they climbed
into bed.
I was left all alone with the thoughts in my head.
I had gone all day long forcing a smile.
Now alone in the darkness, I cried for a while.
I tossed and I turned; I turned and I tossed.

Tears flooded my eyes as I relived your loss.
I wondered once more why God took you away
And left me alone for the rest of my days.
I mourned for my husband, my lover, my friend.
I wept for our romance, its untimely end.
I conjured up memories of Christmases past.
I wish I had known that last year was our last.
My soul felt so broken, my life ripped apart.
I couldn't find joy or peace in my heart.
In the midst of my grieving, I heard your soft
voice.
"Baby, don't cry for me. You should rejoice!
My body is perfect and I feel no pain.
And one day, my Mandi, I'll see you again.
I wish you could be here, and someday you will.
Until then, remember that I love you still."
I turned on the light and I looked all around.
But no trace of you, Rickey, was there to be
found.
Your sweet heartfelt words brought an end to my
tears.
I smiled as your message rang in my ears.
I laid back in bed knowing I'd be all right,
Thanking God for the gift I'd been given that
night.
And I spoke these words as I turned out the
light,
"Merry Christmas, Rickey. I love you,
goodnight!"

The Guardian

Longing to hold you
Fearful to touch
Dying to comfort
Before time passes away
Withering, fading
Even more every day
There's nothing left to hold onto
Yet I can't seem to let go

You were there for me
Protected me
Watched over me

I wanna be your angel

Keep you safe
Hold your hand
Ease your pain
No one needs to go alone

I cry myself to sleep
While I watch you on the couch
So close but yet so far
You need me now
But times have changed
I'm not the girl I once was

Stronger still
Yet weak enough
I can't hold on
It hurts inside
So I let go

And hold on just the same
I won't forget your name
I release my grip and say goodbye
You're watching over me again
This time from on high

In Loving Memory of Our Dear Brother Clifton
1954-2003

On Life & Everything After

I am shrouded in the shadows.
I wonder how long it's been.
I hear a familiar voice calling my name.
I see your mother moving my way, arms
outstretched in an embrace.
I want so much to ease her sorrow, soothe the
pain that fills her face.
I am lost for words, so I simply squeeze her
tightly.

I pretend that I'm okay because I don't deserve
to grieve your loss.
I feel overcome with guilt and burdened by
regret,
I touch your picture in my pocket.
I worry about Mikah living life without you.
I cry until my body collapses to the floor; my
eyes can weep no more.
I am a failure as your forever friend.

I understand Life happens when we're making
other plans.
I say it's one of those things that's beyond my
control.
I dream of one more chance to say our last
goodbyes.
I try to forgive myself.
I hope that you've forgiven me as well.
I am forever haunted, for I discovered in the end,
I was the one who was the "flaky friend."

In Loving Memory of Kimberly, my friend for
over thirty years. May she finally rest in His
peace.

Jana's Song

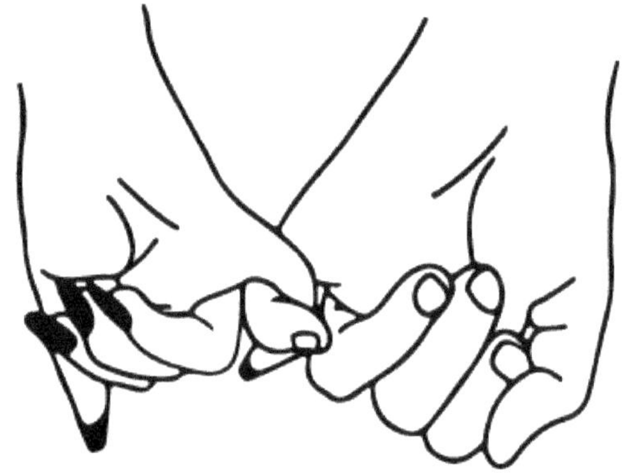

She said, "Hold my hand, Daddy,"
As they walked across the street
She tried her best to match his pace
With her tiny little feet
Walking proud by Daddy's side
Her brown eyes level with his hip
She felt strength and love and safety
With her hand in Daddy's grip
Soon came her first day of school
She was growing way too fast
She smiled up at her hero

Grabbed Daddy's hand, walked into class
The years blow by, she's twenty-five
She's fallen for a handsome man
Who has come to see her father
And ask Daddy for her hand
Their wedding day is finally here
His girl makes such a lovely bride
Daddy grabs her shaking hand
They walk the aisle, side by side
As he gives away his baby girl
His heart is breaking up inside
But Daddy smiles and celebrates
For now, his tears he'll have to hide
The years continue speeding past
His baby girl is now a mother
And Daddy has become Pawpaw
To a sister and her brother
Pawpaw's grandkids are his whole world
They all love to laugh and play
They have so much fun together
Until Pawpaw became sick one day
The doctors ran a ton of tests
They told him he had cancer
He asked how much time he had left
"Not long," came the doctor's answer
As Daddy broke the news to her
He held her hand and let her cry
Though not a child anymore
She wasn't prepared to watch him die

They cried, they laughed, they hugged a lot
And spent every day together
They were making precious memories
So she could hold onto him forever
When that fateful day had finally come
And he could no longer escape Death
She whispered, "Hold my hand, Daddy"
And held on tight through his last breath.

Against Your Will

I'm sorry your life hasn't gone like you planned
I'm sorry you don't think that I understand
I'm sorry you're hurt down so deep in your soul
I'm sorry she left you so callous and cold
I'm sorry your heart has been filled with such
pain
I'm sorry I thought you could be loved again
I'm sorry I can't heal your broken down heart
I'm sorry I don't have a clue where to start
I'm sorry for ev'rything I didn't do
I'm sorry I'm just not the woman for you
I'm sorry I'm not who you need me to be
I'm sorry your heart couldn't learn to love me
I'm sorry your words often fell on deaf ears

I'm sorry we both wasted so many years
I'm sorry my brain works so differently
I'm sorry I can't grasp the things you teach me
I'm sorry I've been such a burden on you
I'm sorry I need you as much as I do
I'm sorry I can't live up to your demands
I'm sorry for asking if we could hold hands
I'm sorry I'm dying to feel your embrace
I'm sorry I'm desperate to kiss your face
I'm sorry my spark doesn't light up your fire
I'm sorry that I'm not the one you desire
I'm sorry for staying where I don't belong
I'm sorry you're right, sorry I was all wrong
I'm sorry we just couldn't see things the same
I'm sorry that you'll never give me your name
I'm sorry you've chosen to wallow in spite
I'm sorry you can't see our love's worth the
fight
I'm sorry your future doesn't include me
I'm sorry it's taken me so long to see
I'm sorry I can't be enough for you still
I'm sorry I've loved you against your will.

FrEeZeOuT

I'd give up my blanket
Just lay here and freeze
To keep you from trying
To get close to me

I'm not wired like you
I can't just flip a switch

And kiss those same lips
That called me a dumb witch

How can I hold you
Or reach for your hand
When your words remind me
How worthless I am

I've tried hard to forget
The cruel things you've said
But they echo so loudly
On a loop in my head

You see nothing wrong with
Words spoken in anger
They don't leave bruises
So where is the danger

Not a scratch on my skin
Has been left by your hand
But your tongue cuts me deeper
Than you understand

I wanted to love you
I gave you my best
Your words pierced my heart
Ripped a hole in my chest

If only you'd shot me

The holes from the gun
Could open your eyes to
The damage you've done

But you'll never see things
Through these eyes of mine
You feel your behavior
Is perfectly fine

You think an "I'm sorry!"
Makes everything right
Like it somehow erases
What you called me in spite

For you, life continues
The status quo stays the same
Meanwhile I'm drowning
In my sorrow and shame
You can't comprehend how
You've shattered my soul
I'm broken so badly
I'll never be whole

Though you've never left me
Laying bloody nor bruised
Don't think for a moment
That I've not been abused

Addicted

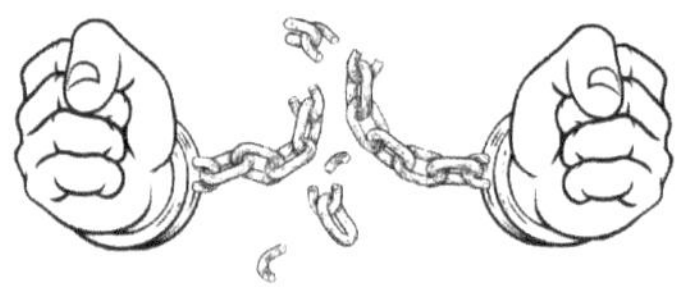

My hands tremble
I can't be still
My body shudders
Against my will
My eyes are wild
My mind is racing
I'm climbing walls
I can't stop pacing
My throat is dry
My lips are cracked
My body craves

What it has lacked
I need a fix
It's been too long
Thought I could quit
Guess I was wrong
I tried so hard
To break away
But I won't last
Another day
I'm overwhelmed
The urge is strong
I've lost the fight
My will is gone
So I succumb
You draw me in
I can't escape
You win again
The one I thought
Could set me free
Will someday be
The death of me

Down the Rabbit Hole

Take me down the rabbit hole
Show me to the other side

Where down is up and left is right
Where ghosts and demons hide
Grab my hand and lead the way
Where dreams and passion thrive
Share with me your secret world
Teach me how to feel alive
Let the dark side swallow me
Invade my brain and snatch my soul
I've dwelled among the light too long
I don't know how to just let go
I crave a freedom I can't claim
I'm bound by responsibility
I long to leave this life behind
Unshackle me and set me free
I want to dwell among the flames
To lose myself inside the fire
To feel it pulsing in my veins
As orange tongues lift me higher
Once I reach the mountaintop
And tumble back down to the ground
When I return to reality
And forget this world we've found
When the embers turn to ash
And the flames have flickered out
Bring me back down the rabbit hole
Remind me what the other side is all about

Crystal Clear

I stare down at the mirror
Overwhelmed by what I see
With bloodshot eyes, I recognize
I'm not the girl I used to be

I catch a glimpse of who I was
She disappears between the lines
I close my eyes and breathe in deep
Just like I've done so many times

I feel the rush, the sweet release

Creative thoughts invade my brain
Amidst chaos, I find my peace
And slowly peel away my pain

I've crossed a line I can't uncross
No shades of grey, just white and black
I'm past the point of no return
For me, there'll be no turning back

Can't be the woman I once was
I fought too hard to set her free
Won't bind her up in chains again
She's gone for good, now this is me

My innocence is stripped away
I'm done with fear, no more self-doubt
I'm brave enough to be myself
It's crystal clear, my secret's out

Hear My Cry

H ollow
E mpty
L onely
P eople
M asquerade
E verywhere

Paranoia

I tell myself to let it go
Ignore the voices in my head
I reach out and remind myself
You're here beside ME, in MY bed
There're other women you could have
And other places you could be
I try and reassure myself
You're here because you've chosen me
I close my eyes and take a breath
I try to set my mind at ease

I wish I could just flip a switch
And kill my brain at times like these
I long to be the things I'm not
Like beautiful and self-assured
I tell myself that I'm enough
Yet still I feel so insecure
Inside my head, I scream aloud
Just trying to tune the voices out
Determined to enjoy myself
And not to wallow in self-doubt
I reach out for your hand once more
So thankful that we share this bed
Your sweet "I LOVE YOU" ends my doubt
As I believe the words you said

Boymom

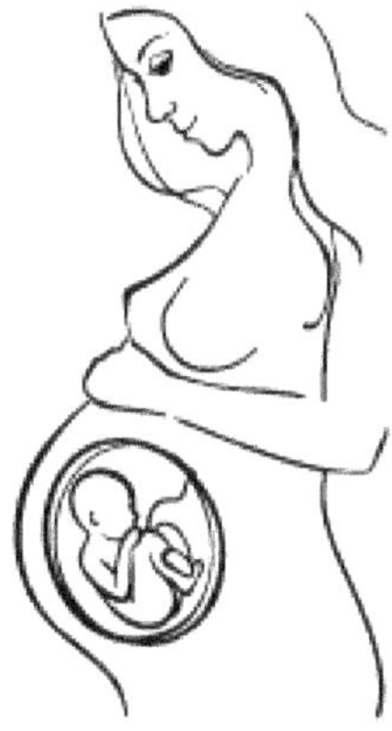

One bright and blazing morning
When the sunlight streaked the sky
The Lord looked down upon you
With a twinkle in His eye
With the angels gathered 'round Him
In a glorious glowing crowd
He laid His hands upon you
As He spoke these words aloud:
Boy moms must be tender
Yet also tough as nails
And discipline their children
With a love that never fails
Not everyone could do this
It takes a special touch

A blend of strength and patience
To love a boy so much
To raise this little babe up,
Help him grow to be a man
To comfort and to guide him
With a firm but gentle hand.
I searched the whole world over
But nobody else would do
I chose you as this boy's mom
Long before you ever knew

The CHRISTmas Spirit

It doesn't feel like Christmas
I just can't get in the spirit
And I think I know the reason
If you really wanna hear it

It's not about the reindeer
Or the old man in the sleigh
It's not about the games that
People gather round to play

It's not about the snowmen

That we build in our front yards
It's not about the carols
Or sending Christmas cards

It's not about the stockings
The turkey or the dressing
What Christmas is about
Is our Lord's special blessing

God sent His son, the Savior
On that ancient Christmas morn
In a humble little manger
Christ the child was born

The wise men and the shepherds
Came to celebrate His birth
Angels spread his joy and
Good tidings o'er the Earth

Somehow through the centuries
The true meaning has been lost
We're caught up in the hoopla
Of how much each gift cost

We focus on the wrong things
Like lights and trees and toys
And telling all our children
To be good girls and boys

We worry 'bout the invites
Or the cards we should be sending
We think about the presents
And the money we'll be spending

But the one thing we've forgotten
Which means much more than all of this
Is the Reason for the Season --
Without CHRIST, there'd be no Christmas!

www.ingramcontent.com/pod-product-compliance
Lightning Source LLC
LaVergne TN
LVHW050938200726
843508LV00011B/2382